alcoholism and depression

SHEILA B. BLUME, M.D.

JOHNSON INSTITUTE

Copyright 1984 © by Johnson Institute, Inc.

All rights reserved. No part of this work may be reproduced in any form without the written permission of the publisher, Johnson Institute, Inc., 10700 Olson Memorial Highway, Minneapolis, MN 55441-6199, 612/544-4165.

ISBN: 0-935908-25-0

Printed in the United States of America

contents

Introduction 5

Depression 7

    Words And Meanings 7

    Differentiating Normal Mood
    States From Illness 10

    Diagnosis Of Depression 12

    Primary Versus Secondary Disorder .. 15

Depression And Alcoholism 16

    Diagnosis Of Alcoholism 16

    Influences Of Alcohol
    And Alcoholism On Mood 17

    Familial Influences In
    Alcoholism And Depression 22

    Diagnosis And Treatment
    Of Depression In Alcoholics 23

**Depression, Alcoholism, And
Suicide** 27

References 28

Introduction

There is a great deal of confusion about the relationship between alcoholism and depression, and the confusion seems to be based on a number of circumstances. First of all, both depression and alcoholism are so common in American society that most of us have had some contact with family, friends, or acquaintances who have suffered from one or both conditions. Also, because they are such common occurrences, there are many assumptions made about the two that are part of our cultural store of "common knowledge." For example, "everybody knows" that alcoholics are people who chase after pleasure through their drinking and feel good when they are under the influence of alcohol. Likewise, "everybody knows" that depressed people drink to cheer up, and many people "know" that most or all alcoholics "get that way" because they start out depressed. Such assumptions have only recently been investigated in scientific studies. Research findings have often shown these "well known truths" to be myths or misconceptions, or at best, to be oversimplifications of rather complex relationships.

The purpose of this work is to clarify some of the concepts involved in relating depression to alcoholism, to provide a brief outline of current knowledge and thinking about these relationships, and to offer a glimpse into the complexity of this subject. If the reader is grappling with a personal or family problem with alcohol or depression, the need for a careful professional evaluation should be evident. Self-diagnosis is only of value as a first step toward obtaining a complete assessment and appropriate treatment. A thorough physical examination may be as important as a psychological one in the overall evaluation needed to develop an effective plan of treatment. Help is available to relieve the pain of both of these conditions. We should no more expect ourselves or others to "snap out of it," "exercise some willpower," or "pull ourselves up by the bootstraps" when depression or alcoholism is present than we would expect a diabetic or a cancer patient to cure himself. Here again "common knowledge" may sometimes lead us astray.

Depression

Words And Meanings

The word *depression,* as related to human beings, is used in a variety of ways in ordinary conversation, covering everything from disappointment to suicidal despair. In medical and psychological parlance, the term *depression* is also used in different ways. In addition, related terms such as *mood, affect, affective disorder, dysphoria,* and *melancholia* have specific meanings important to the understanding of depression.

Depression and manic-depressive illness are generally classified as "affective disorders" because the most outstanding symptoms are serious and sustained changes in *affect*, that is, changes in *mood* and their expression in behavior.

Let us start with *"mood"* and *"affect,"* two of the most important factors considered by a psychiatrist in reaching a diagnosis of depressive disorder. In one standard psychiatric text, *"mood"* is defined as the feeling tone experienced internally by an individual, while *"affect"* refers both to inner feelings and their external manifestations. Thus, it is possible for the mood and affect to be incongruent with one another. For example, a patient who states she feels terrified, but while saying so smiles and appears calm or detached, is said to have an "inappropriate affect." That is, her *affect* (calm) does not match her *mood* (fearful).

"Dysphoria" refers to an uncomfortable or unpleasant internal feeling state. It is often used to refer to depressed mood, in contrast to *"euphoria,"* an exaggerated feeling of well-being.

"Depression" is used in medical and scientific writing in a number of ways: as a description of brain activity, a normal mood state, a symptom, or a diagnosis.

1) *Depression Of Brain Activity*
When used to refer to the brain, *"depression"* simply means a decrease in electrical and neurophysiological activity. The opposite of "depressed," in this sense, would be "stimulated" or "excited." Thus, the neuropharmacologist considers alcohol (like the anesthetics and other sedatives) a "depressant drug." This use of the word *depression* does not necessarily imply any specific relationship to mood. If a person is drowsy, stuporous, or in a coma as a result of a stroke, head injury, or a drug overdose, for example, his nervous system functioning is said to be "depressed," with no specific implication for affect or mood.

2) *Depression As A Normal Mood State*
Depression is also used in psychology and psychiatry, as it is in everyday life, to refer to one of the moods that constitutes part of normal human experience. In this usage, the opposite of "depressed" would be "happy." A range of feelings such as sadness, disappointment, discouragement (what is often known as "the blues"), and sometimes a feeling of mental fatigue, loss of

interest, or numbness ("the blahs") may be included in the term. Such depression is a normal reaction to experiences of separation and loss and is not necessarily a sign of pathology.

3) *Depression As A Symptom*
In medicine, the term *depression* is also used to refer to a dysphoric symptom, that is, a pathological change in mood and affect that may be related to physical or mental illness, or may be the side effect of a therapeutic drug. The opposite of "depression" as a symptom in this usage would be "euphoria" or "mania."

4) *Depression As A Diagnosis*
Finally, the term *depression* is used in medicine as a diagnosis, for example, as in "major depression" or "atypical depression." These diagnoses are among the various classifications of affective disorder listed in the widely used, third edition *Diagnostic and Statistical Manual* (DSM-III) of the American Psychiatric Association. Current diagnostic categories will be touched on below.

"Melancholia" is an old term which has its origin in the ancient theory that all disease was caused by an imbalance of the four body fluids or "humors." Melancholia (meaning "black bile") referred to severe depression associated with a slowing down of bodily functions, often starting in middle or late middle age (so-called "involutional melancholia"). The term is still used in this restricted sense.

Differentiating Normal Mood States From Illness

As mentioned above, a depressed mood may be a normal reaction to separation, loss, and disappointment. Temporary depression may also occur as the aftermath of a long-anticipated happy event, such as a friend's wedding or a special holiday. Depressed affect is observed in normal human infants who are separated from their primary caretakers. It is seen under similar conditions in infant primates and other animal species. Such temporary depressed affect may have the function of acting as a signal to others in the social group that the infant is in need. In adults, temporary depression may also be a signal for help to others in the environment or may be a motivating force within the individual to undertake a course of action which will replace the lost object. Depressed affect is a normal part of bereavement, a process which usually runs its course and gradually ceases.

In evaluating the significance of a depressed affect, the professional will consider the following: severity of the affect, its duration and natural history, associated symptoms, possible causes, and whether the depressed affect is proportionate to life events.

The intensity of the feelings of sadness is, of course, important. Suicidal despair would immediately demand professional attention. The duration and history of a sustained depressed mood is also relevant. Does it fluctuate over time or is it fixed? What are the associated symptoms, if any? Is there loss of appetite, weight loss or gain, loss of sexual interest or potency, feelings of unrealistic guilt and self-accusation, social withdrawal, difficulty concentrating, agitation, insomnia, (or hypersomnia, i.e., excessive sleeping), early-morning awakening with inability to resume sleep, crying spells, or suicidal thoughts? Is there interruption or impairment in the individual's ability to function at school, at work, or in social relationships? Are there delusions (false beliefs) that the individual has a fatal illness or has committed a terrible crime? Is there associated anxiety, with agitation? Is the person immobilized and unable to get out of bed, dress and feed himself or herself?

The professional will also evaluate the relationship of the depression to life events. Was there an important loss with a normal grief reaction, or did the depression come "out of the blue"? Does the mood respond, at least to some degree, to positive stimuli in the environment?

All of these factors, along with the individual's age, sex, family history, subcultural group, and previous medical and psychiatric history are important. In general, a depressed mood sufficiently intense and prolonged so as to interfere with normal functioning should be considered worthy of investigation and intervention.

Physical illnesses, such as certain types of cancer, the side effects of drugs, for example, certain antihypertensives and drug withdrawal effects such as "crashing" after the use of cocaine and amphetamines, can cause clinically significant depression. These possibilities must be considered in making a diagnosis.

Those who suffer from depression include young children as well as teenagers, adults, and the elderly. Symptoms associated with depression will vary with age. For example, the elderly depressed patient sometimes is mistaken for one suffering from organic brain deterioration, because the outstanding symptoms may appear to the family as memory loss, confusion, and difficulty concentrating. In young children and teenagers, conduct disturbances ("acting out") may be part of a depressive syndrome.

At most ages, and regarding most types of depression, women are more likely then men to develop depressive illness. Whether this difference is due to physiological, psychological, or cultural factors, or a combination of these is not yet understood.

Diagnosis Of Alcoholism

Once depression is found to be present as a pathological state, it is currently classified according to the criteria of the American Psychiatric Association's *Diagnostic and Statistical Manual*

(DSM-III). Diagnoses included in DSM-III group of affective disorders are as follows:

1) *Bipolar Disorder* (or *Manic-Depressive Disorder*) is a serious illness which tends to run in families. Episodes include both periods of mania and of depression. Manic periods are characterized by overactivity, over-talkativeness, easy distractibility, grandiosity, decreased need for sleep, and generally speeded-up thought and action. Mood is elated and/or irritable. The individual may engage in buying sprees and unrealistic projects of all kinds. Depressive periods are also severe in bipolar disorder and at times are incapacitating. Manic and depressive symptoms may alternate or occur in separate episodes at different times. Hospitalization is sometimes necessary and long term follow-up outpatient care, with appropriate medication, is usually required. In this form of affective illness, the female to male ratio is closest to equal.

2) *Major Depression* (sometimes referred to as *Unipolar Depressive Disorder*) is a serious depressive episode which may be isolated or recurring, but it is not associated with mild or severe manic episodes. A major depression requires treatment which may be in- or outpatient, depending on the severity of the illness. Antidepressant drugs, psychotherapy, and sometimes electrotherapy may be used.

Both bipolar disorder and some types of major depression may have their origins in disordered brain chemistry. A great deal of current research is concentrating on altered sleep patterns, abnormal patterns of hormonal secretion, and disorders of brain neurotransmitter substances. Neurotransmitters are the chemicals which stimulate nerve cells to discharge energy. Current research promises new and improved diagnostic and treatment modalities for affective disorders in the future, as well as a better basic understanding of human mood.

3) *Cyclothymic Disorder* refers to a somewhat milder syndrome of mood swings consisting of depression and hypomania (that is, elevated mood and overactivity without grossly disturbed relationships with reality). These cases are not sufficiently severe to be diagnosed bipolar disorder. Cyclothymic disorders can usually be treated on a long-term outpatient basis.

4) *Dysthymic Disorder* (or *Depressive Neurosis*) is the term applied to cases of sustained or periodic depression over a long period of time. Outpatient treatment is usually indicated, but inpatient care may be needed at times.

5) *Adjustment Disorder with Depressed Mood* is a depressive syndrome that is clearly a reaction to an identified stressful life event. Symptoms are of sufficient severity to interfere with functioning, or are in excess of the expected reaction to such stress. Many of the milder depressions which respond to counseling or psychotherapy fall into this classification.

6) *Atypical Depression* is a category reserved for depressive syndromes which do not fall into one of the other categories but require therapeutic attention.

Primary Versus Secondary Disorder

In clinical practice, it is not unusual to encounter a patient with two distinct disorders, for example, pathological gambling and major depression. In such cases it is useful to determine which occurred first. The disorder that appeared earliest in time is then called "primary," and the subsequent disorder "secondary." This does not necessarily imply that one of the illnesses is the cause of the other, although there may be some relationship. The "primary" versus "secondary" distinction may be difficult to make if both disorders are longstanding, or if an accurate history is not available. However, differentiation may be important for treatment planning and prognosis, and it is therefore worth the effort expended in trying to determine primary versus secondary illness, particularly in relation to alcoholism and depression, as discussed below.

Depression And Alcoholism

Diagnosis Of Alcoholism

Just as the word *depression* has many usages, the word *alcoholism* also is used in different ways in common speech and in medicine. The ordinary citizen often uses the word to refer to any kind of drinking that is troublesome to society, but particularly to public intoxication. Physicians tend to restrict use of the term. In medicine, "alcoholism" refers to a chronic illness that is diagnosed according to a defined set of criteria such as those developed by the National Council on Alcoholism. The term is used in this booklet in the second, more restricted sense. It covers the DSM-III diagnostic classifications of "Alcohol Abuse" and "Alcohol Dependence."

"Alcohol abuse" is an ongoing or intermittent pattern of pathological drinking, characterized by such features as an inability to cut down or stop drinking, amnesic episodes (blackouts), and drinking despite a serious physical disorder that the individual knows is made worse by alcohol. This pattern is accompanied by an alcohol-related impairment in social and/or occupational functioning. "Alcohol dependence" is characterized by the same pathological drinking pattern and/or impaired functioning due to drinking, plus either increased tolerance for alcohol, withdrawal symptoms, or both. "Tolerance" refers to the need for increasing amounts of alcohol to produce the same effect that was previously achieved with lower quantities. Thus an alcohol-tolerant person may be alert and coherent at levels of blood alcohol concentration which would be associated with unconsciousness in a nontolerant individual. Withdrawal symptoms include morning shakes as well as more severe syndromes such as delerium tremens.

Alcohol abuse or dependence may develop in a person with no pre-existing mental disorder, or there may have been a diagnosable disorder present before the abnormal drinking pattern began. In ordinary clinical populations, most of the alcoholic patients will have developed the alcoholism first ("primary" alcoholism), and a minority will be classifiable as having "secondary" alcoholism—not implying, of course, that the alcoholism was caused by the "primary" disorder. In men, the most common "primary" diagnosis with "secondary" alcoholism is antisocial personality disorder. In women it is one of the depressive disorders. Some authors have referred to this type of "secondary" alcoholism as "affective alcoholism," although the term is not in general use.

Influences Of Alcohol And Alcoholism On Mood

Although most people "know" how alcohol influences mood, there has been surprisingly little scientific study of the subject. A recent review of this research by Mayfield may be found in the book

Alcoholism and Affective Disorders listed in the references on page 28 of this publication. The current state of knowledge may be summarized as follows.

Small amounts of alcohol given to nonalcoholic volunteers does produce some elevation of mood under different experimental conditions, but the effect is small and reaches its maximum at "very mild levels" of intoxication. The mood elevation is reversed with the further intake of alcohol. In other words, "more" is not better as far as an alcohol's ability to elevate mood is concerned.

The experiments that have been performed with alcoholic subjects have generally shown similar results, with mild mood elevation at low blood alcohol levels, well below those sought and achieved during their ordinary drinking. At higher doses of alcohol, and during sustained heavy drinking under experimental conditions, the typical response of alcoholic subjects is progressively increasing anxiety, depression, and social isolation. The depression may reach suicidal intensity. Indeed, alcoholic patients may attempt suicide during a prolonged binge, a state which Mayfield and Montgomery have called the "depressive syndrome of chronic intoxication."

This common state of affairs is familiar to many friends and family members who have observed an alcoholic man or woman during a binge. There is very little happiness or gaiety evident and much pain. Why, the observer cannot help wondering, does he or she repeat such a painful process over and over again? Although the answer is not known, one clue lies in the fact that most of this dysphoria is not remembered by the alcoholic subjects when they are questioned after the experimental intoxication is terminated. Subjects will often report in retrospect that the alcohol made them feel "good" or "better" in spite of the recorded observations of the researchers and their own self-evaluation while intoxicated. It may be, in fact, that alcohol selectively interferes with the recall of the affect. Some recent experimental evidence has pointed in that direction, a hypothesis which may help to explain the complicated events that interact in alcoholic drinking.

Studies performed with severely clinically depressed subjects have shown that mild intoxication by intravenous alcohol did improve their symptoms, yet the behavior of patients with bipolar disorder and major depression does not seem to show that such patients regularly increase their drinking when depressed. In fact, bipolar patients tend to drink more when in a manic phase. If they change their drinking at all when depressed, they are more likely to drink less than to increase alcohol intake.

It may be, then, that patients with primary affective disorder who develop alcoholism later on differ from the majority of such patients in some way, perhaps in their physical and/or psychological reaction to alcohol. At least, these findings cast doubt on such simple formulations as "alcoholics are hedonists who drink to feel good, better, and better," or "alcoholics are all depressed people who get drunk because alcohol is a medicine for their depression."

So far, we have looked at the pharmacological effects of alcohol, that is, the action of alcohol as a drug on mood states in normal volunteers, alcoholics, and patients suffering from affective disorders. Research seems to indicate that a little bit of alcohol elevates mood in normals, depressed people, and alcoholics, but that large amounts of alcohol, especially over long periods of time, tend to cause depressed mood rather than to relieve it. At the same time, recall of how a person actually feels while intoxicated may be specifically impaired later on. Most depressed people do not drink excessively to relieve their depression, although some may do so. Patients with bipolar disorder tend to drink more when manic.

In addition to the drug effects of alcohol, however, one must also consider how the experience of developing the disease of alcoholism influences mood. The progressive loss of control over drinking, the worsening relationships with friends, co-workers, and family members, the repeated failures, and the remorse over behavior associated with intoxication lead to reduced self-esteem, losses of valued relationships, reduced earning power, and prolonged separation from loved ones. All of these life stresses can and do produce sadness, disappointment, discouragement, guilt feelings, despair, and suicidal urges. To these feelings are added the physical manifestations of intoxication and withdrawal, including nausea, vomiting, loss of appetite, incoordination, tremor, agitation, insomnia, and anxiety. Symptoms of alcohol-related illnesses such as pancreatitis and gastritis, and injuries incurred in alcohol-related accidents may occur at the same time, thus complicating the physical and emotional misery of the alcoholic state. In addition, early in sobriety, recovering alcoholics may experience some degree of grief over the loss of their drinking.

There are many studies of patients in treatment for alcoholism that demonstrate high scores on a variety of tests designed to measure depression. This observation of depressed mood is not commonly found in alcoholics who are identified in nontreatment populations — for example, alcoholic relatives of psychiatric patients surveyed in family studies. It may be that depression is the factor that precipitates the entry into treatment for many alcoholics. It also may be that the process of facing one's problems in treatment creates a temporary depressed mood. Perhaps both are true to some extent. In any case, most clinicians agree that the depressed mood seen early in treatment, soon after detoxification, usually disappears within a few days or weeks with continued treatment of the alcoholism. In most cases specific treatments for depression such as antidepressant drugs are not necessary. However, if the depression is severe or suicidal risk is suspected, hospitalization and specific measures may be warranted. Thus an alcoholic who has entered Alcoholics Anonymous

(A.A.) and become abstinent but seems depressed, apathetic, or suicidal should be evaluated by a competent professional and not simply assumed to be going through a harmless temporary phase of early sobriety.

Depression may also occur at later phases during recovery from alcoholism as well as in members of the families of alcoholic individuals.

Familial Influences In Alcoholism And Depression

The relationship between alcoholism and depression may be more complex than implied by such simple statements as: "Some depressed people drink excessively," or "Factors involved in becoming an alcoholic also produce depression." Both alcoholism and depression are known to be familial disorders. There is also evidence that they tend to run in the same families. Relatives of depressive patients — especially male relatives — show an increased incidence of alcoholism in some family studies. In families of alcoholic patients, there is an increased incidence of depression, especially in female relatives. There are a variety of explanations that might account for this relationship. One is that there is a common causative factor, either genetic or environmental, or both, that manifests itself more often as alcoholism in males and depression in females. Another possible explanation is that one of the illnesses causes the other. A third possibility would be that having one of the two illnesses in a family creates an environment which encourages the other. For example, in one study, daughters of alcoholics raised by their own parents had a significantly higher rate of depression than a comparable group of women whose parents were not alcoholics, while daughters of alcoholics who were adopted away early in life did not show an increase in depression. This study involved a relatively small group of subjects, however, and must be replicated before its meaning can be evaluated. Another possible explanation would postulate a third factor in these families, as yet unknown, which would encourage the development of both disorders.

Diagnosis And Treatment Of Depression In Alcoholics

After reviewing some of the known and as yet unknown aspects of the relationships between alcoholism and depression, it will be obvious to the reader that both may coexist in the same person at different stages in the development of alcoholism. Accurate diagnosis of both conditions may be literally lifesaving.

An alcoholic experiencing a prolonged bout of heavy drinking (a binge) may become severely depressed and morose. This person is a suicidal risk and may require immediate intervention. Usually hospitalization is required for detoxification. Suicidal precautions, such as close observation in a safe environment, may be indicated until the patient improves. Unfortunately, intoxicated, depressed people are sometimes jailed instead of being offered medical attention. Disorderly conduct, driving under the influence of alcohol, or public intoxication may precipitate an arrest, and the intoxicated person may undergo an exaggeration of depression and suicidal impulses while in jail. If the jail staff is not alert to the danger, suicide may occur. The typical jail suicide involves a male arrested for an alcohol-related offense, and occurs within the first day or two of imprisonment.

Immediately following detoxification, either on an inpatient or outpatient basis, many alcoholic patients will show depression to some degree. Evaluation of the depression will involve the following factors: intensity of the depression, natural history (i.e., previous depressive episodes, suicide attempts, duration and fluctuation of current depressive episode), associated symptoms, and the availability of stable and supportive social relationships to the patient. In evaluating symptoms, those which would normally be associated with depression in a nonalcoholic, such as loss of appetite, weight loss, insomnia, agitation, fatigue, and difficulty concentrating, must be understood in the context of similar manifestations related to the alcoholism itself and the symptoms of withdrawal. Because of these similarities, the intensity of the depressed mood itself, the quality of interrelationships between the patient and others in the environment, and the presence of intense guilt, remorse and suicidal ideation will be among the important indicators of significant depressive illness. Later on, after detoxification is completed and sobriety is established, the full range of depressive symptoms will be better indicators of clinically significant depression.

Once one of the depressive disorders is diagnosed in an alcoholic patient, it is important to distinguish primary versus secondary depression as defined above. Patients who have suffered depression before their alcoholism developed (primary depressives) may be less likely to recover spontaneously and rapidly from their depressive symptoms. Such patients should be observed carefully both early in sobriety and during the long-term follow-up phase of their treatment. If depression recurs during recovery from alcoholism, early and vigorous treatment of the recurrence will help the alcoholic patient maintain sobriety.

It should also be noted that alcoholic patients who may be classified as "primary affective disorder" and "secondary alcoholism" may not be depressed at the time of their evaluation. However, the need for close follow-up for such patients, with sensitivity to early signs of recurrent depression, is the same as in patients who show depression at the time their diagnosis is made.

Whether or not antidepressive drugs will be indicated in any specific case of depressive disorder in an alcoholic patient is a clinical decision which must be based on overall evaluation by a competent physician. There are a number of types of antidepressants available which are effective in treating depressive disorders of various kinds. It is not always possible to predict which will work best with a particular patient. However, those which have a quieting effect in addition to their antidepressant action are usually the first choice for treating depressive disorder accompanied by agitation and anxiety, while those without such effects are preferred for patients displaying withdrawal and slowing of body functions (psychomotor retardation). These drugs tend to have a slower onset of their therapeutic effect than the neuroleptics (major tranquilizers), so continued observation of the depressed patient is important. Some antidepressant drugs may also produce side effects in certain patients, such as dry mouth and constipation. Fortunately, these drugs have a relatively low potential for producing dependence compared to the sedatives and hypnotic drugs (sleeping pills). However, as with any medication, careful medical supervision and ongoing evaluation of the drug's therapeutic effectiveness is needed.

Patients suffering from bipolar disorder are often maintained on long-term treatment with lithium, which tends to prevent recurrence of the disease. Recent experiments in treating alcoholic patients with lithium have shown some promise, but more extensive trials are needed before any conclusions can be drawn. At present lithium is recommended only for the treatment of those alcoholics who also suffer from bipolar disorder (manic-depressive disorder). Antidepressant drugs have also been investigated as a general treatment for unselected alcoholic patients. They have not been found to be effective.

A patient suffering from both a depressive disorder and alcoholism requires treatment for both. It cannot be assumed that treatment for depression alone will relieve the alcoholism. Moreover, the depression is not likely to respond to treatment until the alcoholic stops drinking. Many years of clinical experience have shown that the alcoholism itself needs ongoing attention if the patient is to achieve recovery.

Depression, Alcoholism, And Suicide

Suicide is a frequent cause of death in both depression and alcoholism. It should be considered a pronounced possibility when one is evaluating any depressed alcoholic patient. Unfortunately, many people still believe a number of "common knowledge" ideas about suicide which are incorrect. It is often said that people who talk about committing suicide are unlikely to act on their threats. Clinical experience has shown the opposite. Expressions of suicidal wishes or plans should be taken seriously. It is also generally believed by the public that when a seriously depressed person suddenly appears to improve, the danger of suicide is passed. This is not necessarily true. It has been found that some severely depressed patients appear suddenly improved as a result of having decided on a suicidal course of action. Thus careful observation and follow-up are a necessity in any severely depressed person. The important fact to remember is that both alcoholism and depression can be successfully treated. We should all make every effort to obtain such help for those in need. There are few experiences as satisfying as helping a depressed or alcoholic person to recover.

References

Solomon, Joel, ed. *Alcoholism and Clinical Psychiatry.* New York: Plenum Medical Book Company, 1982.

Goodwin, Donald W., and Erickson, Carlton K., eds. *Alcoholism and Affective Disorders: Clinical, Genetic and Biochemical Studies.* New York: SP Medical and Scientific Books, 1979.

Weissman, Myrna M., and Klerman, Gerald L. "Sex Differences in the Etiology of Depression," in: Gomberg, Edith M., and Franks, Violet, eds. *Gender and Disordered Behavior.* New York: Brunner-Mazek, 1979.

American Psychiatric Association. *Diagnostic and Statistical Manual,* third edition. Washington, D.C.: American Psychiatric Association, 1980.

Freedman, Alfred M., Kaplan, Harold I., and Saddock, Benjamin J., eds. *Comprehensive Textbook on Psychiatry,* second edition. Baltimore: Williams and Wilkins, 1975.

BOOKS WRITTEN FOR THE NONMEDICAL READER ABOUT DEPRESSION

Depressive Disorders: Causes and Treatment. National Institute of Mental Health. DHHS Publication No. ADM 83-1081.

Depression and Manic-Depressive Illness. Medicine for the Layman Series. National Institute of Health, NIH Publication No. 82-1940.

Special Report on Depression Research. National Institute of Mental Health, Science Reports Series. DHHS Publications, No. ADM 83-1085.

Depression and Its Treatment by John H. Greist, M.D., and James W. Jefferson, M.D. American Psychiatric Press, 1984. This book may be purchased from the American Psychiatric Association, 1400 K Street, N.W., Washington, D.C. 20005.

A Partial List Of Johnson Institute Publications

Alcoholism and Depression
Sheila B. Blume, M.D. $2.25
The Disease Concept of Alcoholism Today
Sheila B. Blume, M.D. $2.25
Off-Beat and Nontraditional Treatment Methods in Alcoholism
Margaret Bean, M.D. $2.25
Drinking and Driving: New Directions
Alexander C. Wagenaar, Ph.D. $2.25
Our Approach To Alcoholism
John Wallace, Ph.D. $2.25
Alcohol and Sexual Performance
Anne Geller, M.D. $2.25
Drinking and Pregnancy
Sheila B. Blume, M.D. $1.75
Alcohol and Adolescents
Margaret Bean, M.D. $1.95
The Supervisor's Role in Early Recovery
Brenda R. Blair, M.A. $1.95
Relapse/Slips
Maxwell N. Weisman, M.D., and Lucy Barry Robe $2.95
Alcohol and Anxiety
Anne Geller, M.D. $1.95
Drink the Winds, Let the Waters Flow Free
Pat Panagoulias and Sharon Day-Garcia $4.95
Chemical Dependency and Recovery Are a Family Affair $1.95
Detachment
Evelyn Leite $1.95
Women, Alcoholism and Dependency $1.75
Making Choices $1.75
Sober Days Golden Years $1.75
Alcoholism / A Treatable Disease .... $ .85
Some Perspectives on Alcoholism
LeClair Bissell, M.D. .... $ .85
Medical Consequences of Alcoholism
Robert F. Premer, M.D. .... $ .85

The Family Enablers .... $ .85
Blackouts and Alcoholism
Lucy Barry Robe .... $ .85
Supervisors and Managers as Enablers
Brenda R. Blair, M.A. .... $ .85
Recovery of Chemically Dependent Families .... $ .85
Intervention: A Professional's Guide .... $ .85
Dynamics of Addition
George A. Mann, M.D. .... $ .85
Why Haven't I Been Able To Help? .... $ .35
Why Must They Suffer So Long? .... $ .35

DATA: Digest of Alcoholism Theory and Application
$25 One Year (4 issues)

The Alcoholism Report $48 One Year (24 issues)

Prices subject to change.

Quantity Discounts For One Publication
50-99 — 10%   200-299 — 20%
100-199 — 15%   300 or more — 25%

For a full list and description of Johnson Institute publications and films, write or call:

Johnson Institute
10700 Olson Memorial Highway
Minneapolis, MN 55441-6199

612/544-4165

THE JOHNSON INSTITUTE was founded in 1966 to work directly with the problems of alcoholism or other drug dependence in our society. From our work with alcohol- or other drug-dependent people and their families, we have come to a clearer understanding of the disease of alcoholism or other drug dependence, have refined some useful methods for intervening with the illness and the accompanying family problems, and have been able to share our knowledge and experience with professional men and women throughout Minnesota, the nation, and the international community.

Johnson Institute services are designed to aid the worker in the field of alcoholism or other drug dependence, the professional in a related helping field, and the interested public:

- *Consultation on alcoholism or other drug dependence for communities, business organizations, schools, and institutions for employee programs, school alcohol and drug programs, and alcoholism or other drug dependence treatment programs;*

- *Training seminars for alcohol or other drug dependence professionals and all persons interested in learning about alcoholism or other drug dependence problems and recovery;*

- *Educational films, pamphlets, booklets, a national newsletter, and a quarterly digest of scholarly information on alcoholism or other drug dependence and family recovery.*